PRAISE FOR *FOUND IN A CONTEXT OF DESTRUCTION*

'If poetry can be an act of recovery, there is not one iota of platitude or solipsism to be found here, and if you think you know where a poem is leading, you will be surprised ... MacGabhann is a writer of tremendous energy and insight, and *Found in a Context of Destruction* marks the arrival of a significant new voice in contemporary poetry.' [illegible] Atkinson

'Vivid, spiky, be[illegible] and this is a stunning colle[illegible]

'The personal realities intimated in these poems would be compelling fare in themselves, but in MacGabhann's hands are rattled for the more venturesome beast inside experience. This is a cracking debut collection from one of our most intense and exhilarating writers.' Dean Browne

'As haunting as it is enchanting, *Found in a Context of Destruction* burns blue with its own potent mythology. MacGabhann has assembled a visceral collection of katabatic beauty.' Gustav Parker Hibbett

'*Found in a Context of Destruction* is a virtuosic debut collection that plays cat and mouse with a self in the throes of addiction and eventual recovery. While the poems chart disintegration and disorder, MacGabhann has remarkable formal control of his subject matter and a deep understanding of the poetic line.' Leeanne Quinn

'Tim MacGabhann's thrilling and abrasive debut collection is an irresistible compendium of oblivions and emptiness.' Billy Ramsell

Tim MacGabhann is an Irish writer who lives in France. His first two novels, *Call Him Mine* and *How to Be Nowhere*, are published by Weidenfeld and Nicolson. His poetry chapbook *Rory Gallagher – Live! – from the Hotel of the Dead* appears with Rough Trade Books. *The Black Pool*, a memoir of addiction and recovery, is published by Sceptre, and his short story collection *Saints* is published by Scratch Books. *Found in a Context of Destruction* is his first full-length poetry collection.

Found in a Context of Destruction

Tim MacGabhann

BANSHEE
PRESS

First published 2026 by Banshee Press
www.bansheepress.org

First edition

A CIP record for this title is available from the British Library.

Grateful acknowledgement is made to Rough Trade Books for permission to reproduce material from *Rory Gallagher – Live! – from the Hotel of the Dead* by Tim MacGabhann, copyright © 2023 Tim MacGabhann. Reprinted by permission of Rough Trade Books.

Banshee Press gratefully acknowledges
the financial assistance of the Arts Council.

the arts council an chomhairle ealaíon | funding literature

ISBN: 978-1-917161-01-5

Set in Palatino by Eimear Ryan
Cover design by Jack Smyth
Printed in Ireland by Walsh Colour Print

'And listen, remember, Dave: *you're* not in here –
it's just your body.'

– Elliott Gould, *The Long Goodbye (1973)*

Contents

Bildungsroman	3
I.	
Caretaker	7
Found in a Context of Destruction	9
The Carpenter's Arms	10
Aubade	11
Guided Meditation App *(First Paywall)*	12
Morelia Ghosts	13
Beeches	18
The Zopilote Above the Hotel	19
Retreat	20
Methadone	21
Twelfth-Stepping the Minotaur	22
II.	
Christmas Ape	29
A Tomb for Sean Bonney	30
Revenant	31
He Goes to the Freezer at Night	34
The Yellow Bittern	35
Bathtub	36
Guided Meditation App *(Second Paywall)*	38
A Mother's Chorus	40
Elpenor	42
A Man Walks Into a Bar	44
Nocturnes	47

III.
Rory Gallagher – *Live!* – From the Hotel of the Dead 51

IV.
Guided Meditation App (Third Paywall) 71
Errata 72
The Detective at Rest 73
Carlos's Grandmother 74
Old Stalker 77
Local Colour 78
A Veteran Speaks 80
Visitation 81
Found Poem 82
After Catullus 85
Guided Meditation App *(Final Paywall)* 86
Nausikaa 88

Acknowledgements 91

Found in a Context of Destruction

Bildungsroman

You need to get out of your head, they all said –
and so I did, got mad out of it,
nine years huffed up in the same brown cloud
as hovered low over the foam of the weir

and lower still above this town with no water
except in that mell behind the power station
where foam spreads nebulae around reeds,
dead gulls, suicidal tomcats, long oil-tentacles –

until the flicked comet of a cigarette butt
lit me up: soft luff and rev, pure ignition,
and what to do then but stutter homewards

through the old Metro's odour of loam
to this street of barred, marzipan-yellow windows,
blue flames, spooned-up silt, dirty smoke lemniscates?

I.

Caretaker

for Beatrice Monti

Home now: flicker-lit
smoke den, corrugated tin.

Alone amid treehush:
hawthorn, fir, ash.

Lightning hit in mute ripples.
The birches dripped tiny falling mirrors,
caught straggle of ponytail, permafried eyes.

When I said yes to the job,
they said *Now you're here to drink,*
not to enjoy yourself, haha.

Watch out for wolves, they said.
Leave food for them. Get them
used to your odour sure.

A pan of mince lay on the step so,
all magmatic sputter and reek.

My first night there I watched
fog creep low over thistle and heather,
listened for their breath in my fire's
muffled thuppeta thuppeta.

Sweet nick of charcoal. Ache in the chest
worse than distance. For a while I couldn't

tell whether I wanted or really didn’t want
the clumped grass to become wet fur:

till one came loping out of the dark
through galaxies of phlox
and I knew for sure.

Found in a Context of Destruction

After we'd been to the looted amphitheatre,
we watched the same beard and nose travel centuries
of emperors' faces across faces of coins
scoured clean of their patina by alcohol.
Acorns' calcium traces had left comets in boar's meat,
and wine tongues kissed over and over in the glass.

The museum captions said a quake knocked two pillars
in a V above the altar, saving the statue for us:
Aeneas's right arm ending in a stub,
his son invisible, Anchises's arms hugging
his throat, eyes empty, needy – a child's.
Rutted tracks the grey of dead coral
lay beneath our feet, beneath the plate glass floor,
beneath cumulus reflected crumbling overhill.

The Carpenter's Arms

That uncle who wasn't an uncle,
his hands on my shoulders,
rain smell breathing from his German army
jacket, sleeves up, the inner fold of one elbow
pink with scarring, stippled, a crosshatch,
thick and webby, all from the needle.

Skinny gallogly, cobalt-eyed prophet
sent to warn me out of my own bad future:
nose the glow of a tabernacle lamp,
beard a half-wrecked Brillo pad, voice a benzo slur.

My father yawped at the pool table – a man
whose bedside bottles breathed the tomcat tang
of who knew how many nights' piss.

That uncle who wasn't an uncle said,
'Do not let us cunts ruin your life.'
Sharky and George scudded past on the pub telly.

I wished I could grab one fin, speed out of view,
but that uncle's hand had my shoulder gripped
while the sad cold of all he'd said
plumed through me, bubbles in the yellow of his pint.

Aubade

The streetlights and security lights make of the dark
a zoo panther, a net-caught gleam made safeish by mesh,

but we're zebras, here on our frameless mattress,
striped by the helicopter peering through the shutters.

The air's charred taste woke me – pollution, the zafrán
of burned tyres, the snow of broken windows

left in sopping heaps after the riot police water cannon.
What will the cops smell like this morning,

gone home to their wives, or to those awful motels
that glow behind the precinct? And whose bodies

will those smells have belonged to first?
And where will those bodies be?

The clock digits and sky are the same dull rust tint.
5.30 a.m. Time to turn on phones, check damages.

Guided Meditation App (First Paywall)

i.

Lie down on bathroom floor
under fan's polar roar.
Tune into slow white howl
of lone car that closes in
and passes on:
billiard ball's long roll
that smoothes a groove of dark
through a zone of frost.
Lattices shatter unheard:
cold smoke blooming
into light-rimmed clouds –
sound made briefly solid.

ii.

Let car howl turn to deep rumble
of tyres on metal bridge amid
whins' tiny fire commas among
the frozen oak and ash. A loose fan-
slat hums: sympathetic vibration
with deep loved gone voice
(pick a name of your own)
unspooling from the radio.
Salt wind. Lake seethrough
nothing colour of saké.
Smoky winter noon.
Basalt sea-gates.

Morelia Ghosts

i.

Red-eyed, wasted, grief-winded,
driving away from the funeral,
my face in the jeep's windscreen
was a dazed, sad child's.

Every sip of hipflask vodka
made steppe grasses stoop
and brush my palate.

I pulled into Morelia
way past the hour of anything good,
stopped at a hotel whose gable end

was lost to a mizzle
that darkened the cobbles
and lacquered them with mud.

Under one lintel,
a lamp-swinging phantom
who'd nipped in for shelter
to rub his skinny arms.

Inside, I drew the curtains,
cabled up for the plunge,
every vein baby-loud and greedy
for poppy-scud, spore-scatter,
that goneness warmer
than the bosom of Abraham.

ii.

The TV showed a late film, some army kid
from a town of smoky-eaved apothecaries,

the art in him pressed out by military school,
when he wished his life would flow like water.
The logo for the TV brand was the Greek god Mercury,
a blotched silver mascot, one finger to his lips.

A sea's shallow vowels played on repeat,
futzed the TV speakers, empty smutched blurts.

A mother and son golf on a cliff, whack out
little bone comets that briefly whiten the night.

That sea's where I'd most like to ebb,
clouds coming apart overhead like brains sent spinning,

the shredded brass of lit rain, the red
plane warning lights at the power plant

blinking me on and off.

iii.

Now a scorpion naps
under the bathroom sink

where little knots of blood
have been fraying up through the water.

A cricket scritches
his little violin

from a shelf above the desk.
Outside, shin-deep in fog,

jornaleros yawn, groan,
kick pebbles

and wait for the jeeps
to bring them to the ranches

where the picking pays double
but sometimes costs everything.

iv.

Skite up the pipe, little spectre,
shard the terracotta tiles,

throw down the flashing
until the pickups turn around

give these men
just one empty day –

and, while you're at it,
because what prayer is full

unless it holds the one praying it,
pick me up in your eely fingers

and drop me into the heart's lake muck,
and let my head nod, a weed underwater,

the tide pulse's amniotic rocking
a thrum in me from boss of skull

to the fat of each toe.

v.

Then bright trolley rattle,
steam, a bucket of tamales
propped on the child seat

beside a long tusk
of styrofoam cups
and a jar of claggy Nescafé –

a mother and daughter team
their giggles a kite
straggling up in brilliant red flags.

Beeches

for Lucía María Treviño

The year you vanished is a headachey syrup,
ink run from receipts piled up like gulls I've shot,
the self a dot and a dash lost
in the valleys of the EKG's jagged Alps.
Outside beech twigs taper fine as capillaries
against bright white nothing. When wind flaps the tarp
over my car their red branches pulse
a set of working lungs. In my dreams tarmac bursts
as new buds' cotton fists knuckle upward
unsocketing cobblestones now they're in heaps
black eggs. O all to kill time till all time thaws
and a day comes when I can walk into the sea thigh-deep
see your jeans puddled on the beach
watch your ghost sprint toward the water's easy reach.

The Zopilote Over the Hotel

for Chris Kitson

Long airborne when I spotted her,
a little cinder-nib drawing zeroes
neater than the grooves in vinyl.

Way up in nowhere, the zopilote
traces out doubled nothings
joined at the ends.

Pool filter drones, slurps, snatters,
gargles, over strimmer-whine,
crunch of grass munched to chaff.

The zopilote's ears are cowled
under a mesh of barbless feathers –
thin, fine, like a microphone's fuzzy hood –

so, for the zopilote, our hotel noise
is swampous wash and backwash:
slabbery static tides, radio squelch, milky swirls.

A buffet hits. She curves, flight
a sudden wild freehand, long-stemmed
zips and loops that slow into a climb she hears

as a tuning dial's skewed whoop
and yaw: then only big revolving
quiet, one thermal blurring into another.

Retreat

This utterance occurs in the room where I hide
to avoid saying *Yes* to the mushrooms
that grow fat and sleek on mountain fog
out of the moss greening the fenceposts.

Locals store these long dark brains in the honey
of cloudy jars, same dark brown as a bog,
spores floating in little pale cottony dots.

Last time I did them was in the home
of a Polish artist who said that all fungi
were alien saviours flowing down in a tide
from outer space. Flying clouds of thistle seeds
thickened the security lights. 'It's weird you're
vegan,' she said. 'Your pores have a meat odour,
like you're *cooking* inside.' Which I wasn't *not*, to be fair.

Methadone

Of all the places your coming clean came undone
the clinic in Ciudad Constitución
takes the urinal cake   that dot lost from most maps

Hot wind billowed trackie bottoms   the cramps
one hanging foot   scuffed dactyls
against the cement   heel sole toe toe sole heel
until head beaten quiet by rhythm

The desert horizon a foil-shimmer   a seashore
you'd hug your chest and rock   as though on a see-saw
until the kick in your gut and that ammoniacal
tang of bad goat above bodiless chuckle

and he'd appear above you   scarier than Ajax
resplendent in his black funeral tux
and you'd puke into the gutter's black leaf slush
till the blue air snowed down thick mercy of a headrush

Twelfth-Stepping the Minotaur

No matter how wasted Carlos got, he'd drop a pin.
The Google Maps line was a red tangle
through alleys more dank with piss-smell
than his mattress. My route was a ribbon-thin
cut on the dark, like those he'd scraub on his arms,
before swabbing up the blood with torn-out Psalms.
'Serve the Lord with fear!' I heard him intone,
which was my cue to check in.

He put his bloody arms out to me –
a kid, suddenly, one who'd grazed his knee
and needed Daddy to come galloping.
'If I stand up,' he said, 'I'll wet myself.'
Easy to hate him. When had anyone helped me?
But then he felt so warm in my fireman's lift.

*

It was dark, and the streetlight was bolloxed.
Tumult of rain turned the road to film-noir Proust.
Loose wires sizzled. My foot caught on tree roots –
eucalyptus, the worst tree, thirstier even than me.
Their growth turned the pavement to a broken ruck
that made me think of Kafka and his ice axe:
maybe a thaw wasn't what he was after,
but a brightly sharded opacity –
a notion slammed in half by my car door.

The storm played theremin wails on the radio.
A concrete siding had burst over Viaducto.
The empty night and the underground car park
were my days on the White Widow – whooshy dark,
all drop and no ground: the heart in me trapped hare.

*

He was in Huitzilac. The road's bends were wild –
past a torched mall, past a historic bell
rung by some lad before he was shot to hell
by the army, and past a lake that held
a drowned town under its waters.
The cupolas floodlit white as chalk.
In my head, the towers snapped like poppy stalks,
left juts of masonry like broken molars.

I parked under eucalyptus: the worst tree –
such thirsty roots, sap like napalm
seeping through desert-camo bark.
The moon was a bottle lid pinged through the dark.
My chest twanged for bordeaux and Valium,
the need a mell of tadpoles wriggling through me.

*

My first year clean, I'd hide in bed,
missing the drink-spins, dreaming I was a bin bag
loaded with rotten mangoes, waking with a gag,
sinking darts into the soft of my head.
Everybody's mouth was a zero that made noise,
just endlessly subtracting. I'd pray
for the blare of earthquake-warning tannoys,
for gas to flare under every tree,
row after row, the boulevard ablaze,
as though jet-strafed, because I couldn't see
a future without the bad voice in me
rumbling open my sagittal suture
and skittering me straight to the boozer,
where I'd freeze before the bar mirror's Medusa.

*

Those bad days weren't as gone as I might want:
the wakings, bloody-knuckled, in a schoolyard;
the wine-bubbles thick as frogspawn; my prayer
of *Let this thing in me lie down and die for once*
never, even for a second, answered;
the alchemy of bad pills igniting as good pills,
their sudden lightning opening floors
into squares of dazzle; crying for no-one,
crying only when my brain was walnut-dry,
squeezed free of all necessary chemicals.
Rap my sternum: the sound's air blown
across the top of an empty bottle,
because dinner was the bath that I ran
and slid into, water pressing down hunger.

*

Nine years in fifteen-minute tape-loops:
the early house's cherry-red beer taps,
neon smoors all night, morning's brassy glare,
the morning soundtrack a freight-train rattle
numbed to a rumble by the day's first bottle,
then noon sleeps, so cushiony with stout, the quieter
and the darker for there being zero stars.

I'd picture myself as an old rosary
wound around fingers that have lost their bones
but kept their nails and hair. Dust caked my filigree.
My Jesus was deeply flayed by corrosion.
Light would spill down the bricks of my crypt,
and God would lift me out for a check and a sniff,
say, 'You've a ways to rot yet', then drop me again.

*

My walk to the square: a trailing clitter
of almond husks dropping to the ground.
From here, the map's red line snarled around
a row of parked trucks. Cottony flocculence:
thick counterglow. Frowning eaves of warehouses.
Drizzle left no-worth pearls on my coat sleeve.
Violet light fell from the San Judas altar –
a gilt pod, decked with candles and gerberas,
his gaze so sure I felt like I could leave
the earth by grabbing the hem of his robe –
in an oval of flickering mist over

Carlos, lying prone under Frito packets –
so still: too still. The blood beat in my teeth.
But then he yawned. I breathed out. The light strobed.
'What are you *wearing*?' was all I could muster.

*

Buckled cardboard horns were taped to his forehead,
dirt and loose hairs stuck all over the Sellotape,
over a bull-mask dinged half out of shape.
He looked at me and groaned. 'Halloween,' he said.
Around each iris was a maze of veins.
Lifting him, he was lighter again –
he'd been drinking his sleep, smoking his meals.
His smell poured bad pictures through my skull,
but the map took us over cobblestones
and through memories of me and my father
eating Creme Eggs and reading the *Beano*
on the bonnet of his car, back from somewhere
grey and marshy, among birches the colour of bones,
but safe now – the sky dark, the lamps solder-yellow.

II.

Christmas Ape

i.m. Horacio Warpola

How cool would it be one bright morning
when this life is not quite over to wake up
and pad, slippered, along the corridor's
unechoing red carpet pocked all over
with tiny diamond eyes pupiled with black,
and in the sitting room find, one arm
draped over the couchback, the other
at rest across the leathern craquelure
of his belly, an adult male orangutan
staring not quite blinklessly past the tree's
lit tinsel, into the swirling of the sleet.

You might ask him, 'What're you watching?'
and he might say 'Nothing', or nothing,
only point, and you might sit together
in radio-free, TV-less silence, amid citric
tang of dying pine, and head pictures
might roll through both your skulls showing
blasted taiga: black spruce, infinite snow,
a page whose letters have all blown over.

A Tomb for Sean Bonney

after Mallarmé

If it ends in petrol, rags, and ice,
can we keep you here in a single, flung bottle of smoke,
its blast tinting the bellies of the pigeons

and bursting through the window
to go off in a mud star of melted plastic
across the god of love's fifty-inch flatscreen?

The funeral roses you'd like, I know,
are the pluming reds of the bomb
under every cop-shop desk.

You were made for ground war –
Anubis-headed snuffler through sewers and their tomb-smell,
their slaver of rubies and muck.

Heart eater, cougher of smashed glass, we'll breathe this air for
    you
till we're dead of it, and forever remember:
What has no guts but swallows everything? The police.

13 Nov 2019

Revenant

i. Tommy's Ghost

He was a shape out of the mud steppes.
One stool over, voice skewed and whorled
like an AM radio ghost, warming his hands

over the coal-red glow of the Bud taps.
He let his clabbery loafers swing and catch
against the carpet's red nap. 'I made it out.

I left a decoy tombstone: my oar, flaking away
over no body. My worst scar is this white zero,
right where I spiked my heel on the tine of a gate.'

Cords the white of sinew showed through.
The electronic poker machine glowing bloody
in the corner breathes the feel of a ferry casino.

He says, 'I burst my road out. In the hills lived
stone blunt people and shut faces.
Their burned poems' smoke climbed me.

I only read the lindens' buckled letters to the air.
Lopped early, their stumps shine with sap.
Think of it: a snowfield page of full stops.'

The drink currents chase past my toes.
Ethanol heat keeps me from the freeze:
not from the black speed he gave me.

ii. Tommy's Drown

The stout in a black tide eeled down lead steps after him.

Down he was drawn then to the clear sea. His walrus eyes
went big and salt.

The broken SOS of his last neural blastings. All last words end
dot, dot, dot.

Difference between you and me? Thirty years and one narrow letter.

Tumbled end over end he smacked hard off the heads of the
groynes on the flooded beach.

The currents that sped him were a raft of eels.

Ferry lights' yellow oil spills way out. The river dives to the
estuary.

Currents' bunched lines craze into nothing: a page that's
learned to shed letters.

iii. Tommy's Prayer

O and all I want's to be serene in linens
on the white shore of a rum bottle label;
for my eyes to brim silver happy zeroes,
for me not to tumble among sharks,
and that there would be my prayer done.

He Goes to the Freezer at Night

and holds his ear to the cloudy dark.
He's chosen to hear it as *ferocious*

at the liver, which leaves argument open
as to lines of causation. Yes, yes, I know:

you never got to be a kid, found
your mother-in-lieu when the bottle's cap-
hoop rang cleanly as it spun:

and then the glass, the whisper of juniper,
enough to still all skull murmur – those old
horror sutras, their mutter set to repeat.

Yellow Bittern

after Cathal Buí Mac Giolla Ghunna

When I came upon your downed neon
amid flinders left by holidaymakers
in the beach's pelt of marram grass
I had to kneel and shoo the ants
off you: their black caviar glisten
was no worthy offertory altogether.

I clicked my tongue, wished I'd gotten
to you in time, poured an acorn
full of lake water into the pink satin
lining your beak, felt your heart putter,
felt you kick free into high blue nothing.

Bathtub

for Hassan Hamad

What words for when I saw you,
curls abob and wobbling, plaster
dust pattering down from them,

your colleague's baffled
one-finger hoke
through the floppy shoebox.

I'll stop. You know how it was.
Instead, let me give you more
than nearshore water's

hoosh and hush, more than
estuarine rushes, their smell
of river water meeting sea.

We could cross sand
and alluvium, wet grass
darkening our chinos.

Each fogged breath's
frost taste could dab
the burned tar scorch

from your lungs and throat.
You could pick out a star froth
of flowers in wisteria's

unbroken lacework.
You could chill on a rock.
I'd rip drizzle-wetted moss

thick as gauze from that rock,
offer to dab your eyelids.
But why stop there?

Take my place, brother:
claw-footed bath, wallpaper
with candy stripes, knuckle

scalding heat, bright water
from the taps. The thud, dunt,
whump you hear is just pipes

waking up. Bountiful glug, water
on water. Rain patter on jasmine
gardens whispers now: *Release*.

Guided Meditation App (Second Paywall)

iii.

If in airport hotel rub ATM receipt
between finger and thumb
till whorls of tips go smeary grey
and their rustle becomes a fizz
that makes you see white water
and effervescent black foam
whose every bubble forms the hoop
of a zero. Thick wet haze creeps over
parked cars outside. Let videogame
elsewheres rise in your head:
Spain, Japan, an America
of tenements and fire escapes
whose staircases are piled up
frazzled scores
for harpsichord. And yet
you will remain all glitch and jitter.

iv.

Now dream the storm outside
into an immense radio
whose every squiggle and twist
of radio fuzz and tuner-keen
is a small lit boat on an ink sea
that you're watching from the shore,
a flat stone in each hand. The fan
overhead has retuned itself,
slowed into a semibreve

beat your heart and lungs
can catch up with now,
peering into the amber
dimness of the aircon
grid, toward the wafer-fine
chopped up shadow
of the fan going around.
Smoky winter noon.
Basalt sea-gates.

A Mothers' Chorus

What they did to us   *no worse than we dreamed*

Now we fly as a squad   a big wind of atoms low to the ground

All we do   All must together do

The tree my daughter   *used to read under*

never thought she'd say   *goodbye to it*

Back from the death pit   from the black door

Back from under the cornices the volutes the mouldings all bitty and rotted

Back from that riverless city where the police chased us down

Back from the ambulance   Back from the back of the riot van

Back from our heaps   in the garbage truck

Dead in the driveway   *I watched my son's shape drip*

over the edge of the rearview mirror   Back from the cliffs

we were flung off in milled bagfuls Back from the wave we were

sifted into sand billows   Little nibbles of fish kisses

When my daughter was lifted   *I saw towers falling*

Back from pine logs the scattered leaves Back from that pyre in Hidalgo

Fat spatter louder than rain on one million candles

Snatched at midnight from streets she won't walk again

and that I have to Back from the calligraphy of hairs

stuck to wet ceramic Back from ash finer than wind

caught alamo seeds a helical mania Back from gutter rain's

carbonated gargle Our throats going *No more*

I just want God to tell me what names to curse

As far as here this room this brassy strike of light turning

A pollen grain above old maps all lines wiped off

Elpenor

Wine-tone light over the wreck of the castle
and wine smell warmed from dead pine needles
drifted against us two, panned out on our backs
under the last of the sun.

A man on TV ignited in the stern of a boat –
lit chrism of petrol, blue-edged, rolling
from dome of skull to ball of heel,
caping him, crowning him, lifting him above us.

You'd had a dream that made you feel okay –
your own heart, wet, steaming, sheathed:
a tamal in a corn leaf.

'My index finger slit open my own breastbone,' you said,
'like a laser, as easy as that, melted apart, zip zip,
but leaving my finger lipsticked with clots of red.
Beneath, I saw the meat of me was all spiced and dark.
One layer down again were bees,
fossicking rot into clean, sallow wax.'

While you'd seen all this,
I must have been in the shower,
swabbing myself with a loofah
of wadded-up liver-coloured banknotes,
and slicking myself with the leakage
of their inks: a bloody foam,
and a steam thick as incense.

That slap of suds on tiles
was like applause for the arias pealing
out of my phone's custom alarm setting –
The Magic Flute, that version of *Turandot*
with the happy ending swapped in.

A Man Walks into a Bar

Interview Location: POSADA LA PRESA, TEPOZTLÁN
Recording Date: 9/1/16

[thick slap of pool water against tiles, filter drone]

'For years I've tried to find life less dear to me:
the trails from plantation to cave to palenque so cold,
little in the libraries, less in the streets.
But now and then you can taste Africa –
salsa de cacahuate, stewed mats of acelga,
lard-fried triangular corn cakes, just like the South.
One day at the market pictures rose from my plate:
my father over the skillet, Sunday morning,
tossing cracklings, from Queens via his tastebuds.
On my way back, my elbow bumped a goat's skull –
skin gone, eyes empty, every tooth sallowed by the fire.
Happier here? Who knows. Safer? What's *safe*?'

[a strimmer whines, branches crunch]

'By day, on the balcony, above the pool
reflected light flashes in helices from water to tile
while a fire makes birds' bones of the hilltop firs.
At night the fat pads of an iguana's feet
go clapping up along the brick.
He may well want nothing of me –
to slop a bowl of water, gobble some papaya,
to roll the seeds along his tongue like ants.
But I don't want to see him, not at all,
not the S-shapes that his shadow makes,

not his floppy, skull-to-tail mohawk of wrinkles,
not his eyes like lithographs of a dead man.
Scorpions sneak into my socks sometimes, die, dry,
skitter like rosary beads across the floor
next time I unroll a pair, but that's all, really.
Caught in a storm once, I ducked under a bridge,
wound up saturated regardless. Too wet to care
how heavy a zone this was for a man of my tone
I found a bar – mildewed brick, blue neon, banquettes.
A grin licked all around the room.'

[a long sigh sends up a foily burst of static]

'Barman's big Irish head called me *sir*, giggled.
Nobody was talking. Everyone was watching.
Cop memorabilia hung on the walls:
helmets, coshes, rust-blotched old photos.
When my old fashioned slid across the bar, my eyes
were locked on the optics, on a glass case
behind the green gleam of Hennessy and Jameson –
time-cured nubs spread in a ring on green velvet,
way they'll sell you shark's teeth in tourist ports.
The barman leans in, his face a Halloween red glow,
says to me, thumb aimed at the ring, *Friend of yours?*
A bead of wet rolled down my glass, down my back.
The giggles sizzled into chuckles, burst as laughs.
Those darkened rounds were knuckle bones: a human trophy.'

[shallow clatter: fat ice cubes in glass]

'How I got out? I don't remember.'

[contemplative crunching of ice]

'One week later came my first visit here.
First man I see is a blind guy toting an accordion
and I have to blink frames of my dad's town,
mothers queueing to frame their daughters' diplomas,
clack and whoop from pool halls late at night, tamales,
do-nothing Sundays, beer crates, old folks' cane chairs.
This town is Gaspar Yanga's last known whereabouts.
See him in a half-gone engraving on a cantina wall,
two numb eyes, blank as two musket muzzles.'

Nocturnes

Lampshade's glow after eleven:
the lilac veins of her cat's ear –
a bell of light to curl up inside.

*

Beached, speechless,
watching you Sharpie
a sun, moon and stars
across the arse of your latest.

*

Compersion 101: make me lick from your nape
the cherry lip gloss left by last night's locum tenens.
Crushed glister, starmush, pinkish syrup slick.
Let sparkles clag under tongue and coat throat
till a smoky whimper coaxes itself from the larynx.

*

Last tram: Anubis
in uniform rumbles
a cargo of empty light
home over the rails.

III.

Rory Gallagher – Live! – *from the Hotel of the Dead*

i.

I tell you this in a voice in whose tarry gargle
even I can hear whiskey nights
and morning-after stout restarts.

I tell you this because my throat's too flittered
to sing it   my fingers too stodgy on the dots
to tell you in anything bigger than words

My poor guitar is nearly finished
each ding and dunt and scar and dent
the illegible scribble of every disaster

the fretboard stain-whorled with fingerprints
the dark pucks of pulled off skin chunks

that fleck the neck
from too many gone awry glue-jobs

Scratchplate hangs by one screw
and many prayers   the wood
hatcheted away   by pick action

In the curved back   my jeans' folds remain imprinted
enough for you to think of fossils left in mudstone

My hands have holes gone out of them –
all the home repair solder jobs

The only story is what's written in damage
and regaled in the blue waul
near the twelfth fret   mids way up

Translate that   you can keep my biography

ii.

Talk of the quake in Mexico
two thousand troops on the streets
bulldozers pulverizing the Costurita plant

on the hotel-bound car's radio
through an absolute pea souper
radio news humming the radiator slats

How the guitar case shunted
down the carousel
at the airport
nubbled surface rivered all over with rain

made me think of a new coffin
that I might ride along canals
thick with reeds and wet clay smell

My stagger to the door a rescue donkey
wobbling stunned
through the wreck of a market

hauling a cart of rubble

iii.

On the hotel telly divers plunge
through undersea murk

torches carve the dark
towards guardrail metal
so rusted and weed clad
it could nearly be coral

and I see me and the band
as we'd look should a goose fly
beak first into the engine slats

us there skeletons belted to seats
drifting apart bone by bone
our maraca clack muted
by miles of salt water

iv.

Next channel:
Elliott Gould at sea

feet cart   wheeling
a mad thrash
heels find only sand billows

Next thing he's chasing a car
tie whipping forehead dripping

then floored cruciform
on the tarmac   horn blare
rainbow dazzle of headlights

v.

Head pictures last longer than people
a clockface against a blue night
an ache to the green-tinged streetlight
spilling over brick

Her almond and new-soap smell
a pale smell I'd untangle
through clouds of cider and Drakkar Noir
through front-row fug and alleyway piss

through the hundred hours I'd spend
cleaning the violin-curlicues
on the vamps of my boots with a pin
nicked from my ma's sewing-box

then pegging it over to hers
my steps braked against the camber of our road
to make every sun hit moment stretch as far as it could
before they'd snap
count every poke of scutch grass
count every celandine that bobbed in the verge

vi.

At the jacks sink
trying to rinse her from my head
but the tap's cold-water sting
jets me the whole way back
to the mannerly freeze
of her parents' house
a numbness humming in my teeth

vii.

Security lights briefly sepia the walkway
rain's phosphor seethe spills of fern and sword plant
banana leaves baskets of creepers
five-floor tall palm trees in their orange lagging of ivies
Orb lamps an angler fish glow

and a white grand piano galumphs down into the pool

bubbles wobble big as jellyfish

out between the keys the lid on it a drowned sail flapping

viii.

My father helped build Ardnacrusha Dam
guided me and my brother one day
around the slabber the sand the heaped up gravel
up a clay ridge to look down into
the C-shaped sections of tunnel
booming echoes glaring discs of light either end

He died in an estate of plaques hung
above dead lilies in jam jars and cans of Bass
with Gaddafi getting the honour guard
from a balaclava'd cohort
up there on the gable-end murals.

He'd a car seat for a couch
and nothing in the fridge
only a lick of butter
with mouldy breadcrumbs
that I'd to flick out with a knife

He'd watch snooker
on a banjaxed black-and-white telly
because he'd managed to learn the greys

ix.

An accordion player after a pub sesh
showed me the two harvest moons
printed in either side of her forearm
where a UDR dumdum went in and out of her.

'I heard a corncrake chatter, felt the stab
of a red-hot poker, hit the ditch,
sure for a long time I was dead
till caught rain fell from the brambles,

pattered down over my face.' Driving home,
a patrol stopped us, reefed through our gear,
let us on, shaking like Bargaintown wardrobes.

When we were not quite out of sight
I rolled down the windows, let my bare arm
ride the gusts all the way back south.

x.

And just that pure velocity
slowly blowing my mind
no click of seatbelts
no shunting gear
no brake-jerk of arrival
the lads puck talk back and forth
a no-stakes frame of pool
cigarette smoke turning there
a net underwater

Heaven could be that:
hurtling tour-bus motion
the swoop in the gut
like a dive off a bridge
that lift under the ribs
a raking zhoosh
a jump in the feet
and the tunnel lights' white blur
a make-believe of flight

xi.

The blues won't leave much of you
when you get to the end

A tattered lagging coats my walls –
photos snipped from LP sleeves
and magazines, Sellotape strips
mealy with years of dirt.

Muddy Waters. Jimmy Reid.
Blind Tom Wiggins. Blind Lemon
Jefferson. Blind Boone. Leadbelly.

xii.

And there in the centre pudgy and grinning
pencil-tached Lenin hat cocked back

Muddy Waters looking like the right way
to grow old He called me once before he died
talked about Albert King's guitar tone

Voice warm with envy: 'That blue, that strong, solid,
fly killer blue – that pre-dawn tint you get in you
in the long wait after closing time: for check-in,

for check-out, for a plane, for a train, for a bus.
That huge high lonely. Maybe I caught it no more
than four notes at a stretch. Maybe that's all.
Maybe I'm not very human, but that's all I ever wanted.'

The night he died I lit a rake of tealights
splayed his album covers out like wings
three by three propped them on their ends
in front of the telly split edged envelopes
with faded colours every picture I could find
tried to multiply him out across the place
he'd been subtracted from

xiii.

Plane dreams: tundra borderland
no troops around   the river before me
all the old barbed wire snapped by rust
black lines against white sky   a stave
each cut knot a crotchet   a quaver   a sharp
and quiet   and stillness   I've got zero need to break:

and then buffets of turbulence
take the floor from the world
and I take a Bruce Grobbelaar knee-slide
to catch the dead formicary of ash and cig butts
contained in a tumbling bottle of slivovitz

Hangover's tom-tom thud
from night-before-the-press-shots shots
and the heartbeat tick tick tick in my glottis
like the croc that swallowed the watch

After the belt and the tremor shook
in my seat till I thought I'd have
every bolt shook from the plane's
fuselage   slowly then though pill-lull
made a pacified zone of my head

xiv.

Mid-show battery dead all of a slap
the backstage coffee's jump leads useless
drink-tides bobbing the heart

the frown could pass for focus
the grin could pass for peace
no matter how dry my teeth feel

battened tight to the Strat
an otter hugging a twist of driftwood
in swirl upon swirl of foaming stage lights

But then a bright wordlessness drops
the show's commotion total   an ocean
song a coracle hopped

over and over the waves
scales climbing all around   plumes of vapour
the beat neither forward nor backward,

and me above it   abiding in the roar
sweat's brine-spray

and the instant crashes

leaving me home   gone   nowhere

xv.

Used to be I'd dream of a chord so steeped in gain
as to pancake every peace wall, fray every bale of wire,
prise helicopter rotors backwards like fingers,
fire screws out of every jeep's armour plating,
and avalanche brick chunks and powdered mortar
over every British soldier.

Now it's sea dreams that get me when I'm playing,
dry ice thick as coastal haze dark around my ankles,
the sea-thoom of bass, the cymbals in wave-crashes,
and the anemone-armed crowd reaching for me
through the jellyfish purple of the lights.

xvi.

People are hard on the stars who disappear
The charts are as cracked as I'll get them
short of a synth and gleamier chompers

A life without glory   that's my plan

Glory's when the stage-fright retch kicks
like a horse in your guts
and you don't hit your own Redwings

I like the taper in the word *isthmus*
land ending in a dash
or a basalt ellipsis   either will do

Let that hyphen in stone
be a breath taken in
with no uptake expected

slick rocks   wee dribbles of seawater
the view rising in the form
of a horn section's plunging blare
a ruined cathedral opening in my head

heart going ninety   triple-time hi-hat quavers
snare-and-cymbal spinal tingle   salt blood rush
breath-surge joining white points of lens flare
sinewave shapes and the unplayed lead line's last gull-wheel

till last slow downward climb
along ocean-softened rock
into fog   a hail of ions   and nothing else

IV.

Guided Meditation App (Third Paywall)

v.

Allow the switched off flatscreen
to become an inverse canvas
depicting the curves of dormant
volcanoes whose rims are edged
with the iridescences of early
morning. Big loud words only:
this is a dramatic landscape.
So – magenta, tangerine, great
polar shivers of Kodachrome blue.

vi.

If you wake at two a.m.
watch the thrashing of a fir
under the white glare
of the security lights
become three or perhaps
even four independent
storeys of movement
that shake in separate,
like a brush that takes away
one layer of paint each go
until all that's left
is a throb of cloudy absence.

Errata

Not my bow but my laugh made the hall
ring with a swallow's note. To see them all
panned out puffy and hungover got me tender
but not so much I didn't sizzle one lad's arse
with a power hose. The others scarpered.

*

My son brought the buckets and the Harpic.
If I could, I'd have scalded my brain empty
of all the bad war pictures with bleach, hot suds,
made a ringing cleanness of my veins' flumes.
The spongers got spongeing. I went upstairs.

*

Much later, I asked my wife to spin her deadpan yarn
about my last voyage, my tomb under an oar's cracked plume
so we could keep poets and autograph hunters off the trail.
Her tears alone were real: didn't matter that I'd returned.

The Detective at Rest

I miss the pre-arrival feeling
of car wheels, curves of mountain road,
town's glitter dots through low cloud,
each yellow speck a boat nearing port,
and warm arms spread to meet
the hiss of the bus doors.

But the meteors really gleam here –
atom-light million-year-old tonnages,
matter clarified by heat and speed
into long, combed streams of light.

I've had no post in months
and I bump downhill,
one arm loaded with firewood,
the other reaching for fogged out trees
whose trunks are rungs
for a ladder of smoke.

Carlos' Grandmother

Interview Location: HOLIDAY INN EL PASO
Recording Date: 30/12/12

[TV noise: audience applauds, Elvis Presley mutters his gratitude]

'Last time I saw my grandmother
she asked me
to roll her a cigarette
from the garden.
She held up her kinked fingers.
I can't anymore.

And like, this was a whole thing.
She'd say she saw light
criss-crossing on the floor
as though thrown off lake water
coming through leaves
of the tobacco plants,
the beanstalks, the potatoes, the calabacitas –
and they weren't even there anymore.

Plus, you know, she was still funny.
When I brought her a cheese this one time,
she just moved her eyes
over its big moon-crater pores, said,
Everybody is being so kind. I'm worried.

So I figured she was laying a prank on me
with this whole cigarette thing.
And so I slipped out,

meaning to slit open a Lucky Strike
and spill the brown shreds into one of my skins for her.
Subterfuge can be kind sometimes.
Plus, you know, I might top her joke.

But there it stood, a swaying green miracle:

the same stalk my grandad would fondle
and pull wet leathern braids from
to leave parching on the boards of the porch

while he filled his ears with the bright gauze of the air:
bird chitter, cicada shirr, dripping miles of pines,
his radio burbling out the football.'

[lighter clicks, the wet sputtering of a bong]

'And I mean, you know, I shouldn't have been surprised.
All sorts went on there.
Grandma used to grow these orange chiles in a clay pot
to fatten on bad arguments caught in the air.

She chopped them into carnitas once, out of spite,
but the pot burst open to warn her husband,
spilled black dirt across his plate.'

[click of a can, Zippo scrapes then flares]

'After he went, her room became an El Greco sometimes,
hearts crowned with fires ringing his head

as he knelt to kiss her forehead, a living painting.

So the hank of tobacco draped on the porch rail
no me sacó de onda. I just fibred a root-fine twist
of the stuff into a skin, licked shut the fold,

took the lit rollie back in, and pressed it to her lips.'

Old Stalker

Ghostlight in the birches.
The driveway's black serif
unkinks into pure white fog.

Easy to imagine a lone, lost
mummer adrift and stumbling
towards the glow of my door,

doffing his straw mask's mucky
tatter to lay bare a cured
turnip head, the homodont

underbite jut, the split-coak black
of two eyes lodged under
a seamed forehead. He longs

for disassembly, parts laid clacking,
loose as ninepins in a pine barrow,
but nobody yet has looked for long

enough past the fright of his eyes
to appease their affrighted sparking.

Local Colour

i.

At once make-believe buccaneer
bundling home at last: and what I am –
tired self-salesman juddering down

the last speedbump to forty,
smoothing his hands across
the bar top's sallow saddlebow,

then folding arms before the telly,
Brighton versus whoever, it's all
the one delayed island transmission

intended to remind those onboard
that the land behind's still there,
and isn't just a trick of those lights.

ii.

Boat engine's rumbled lullaby
shudders the balls of my feet.

Armchair a pleather nest.

Wind's bad uilleann pipes flutter
scales up and down the chimney.

Anthracite with a soft dooft
collapses in the bar's hearth.

iii.

The plan, *the plan*: rustle up
guts of a deposit, thereby

buy coffin, watch hail,
not bombs, cosily strafe town;

mooch forever after between
home and a glassed-in terrace

within earshot of seawash,
within sight of saltcrash.

iv.

My shape wobbles at me
in the window: hand to mouth,
eyes emptily agog.

A floundering knowledge
of how bunched I actually am:
smother-quiet, thick as coaldust.

A Veteran Speaks

Interview Location: [redacted]*, OVENTIK*
Recording Date: 16/6/16

for Balam Rodrigo

[rain-mutter, fluted utterance of wind in flue]

Winter quilts deep into July,
bunkered down among book stacks,
note-heaps, chocolate bars' dark ingots,
timing my iambs to the lonely morse
that plinks from the balcony's metal struts

until a door opens from here to '94,
back before my voice wore itself hoarse,
back before all the old platitudes
got cratered, blasted, sharded,
marl-dripping cobbles flung at riot cops.

[drops plink from gable end; sudden rainsurge wallows over the static]

Visitation

for Aixa Rava

Rain sloothers down, grooves forest-floor clay
and its fibrous black pelt of smushed elderberries
till a cured shoe leather smell rises
around the honeysuckle's deep narcotic
gold – still hanging on with the hawthorns
well into November. This green murk
low upon the alders is a horror film
but with a plot twist: the monster's been
benign this whole time, so you're the villain.
Any minute out here the rain crackle
on beechmast and dead leaves
could become shakers and maracas
that charm down a striped red whale
out of the heaven of her killed mythology
to go lowing again through rain like smoke
even though there's no one left to hear,
no one left to get it, no one, nothing only
this future of plains reclaimed
by a sick ocean, where rusted containers
flake soundlessly apart under tonnes of water.
Let box retail leak and free a pink smoke
of unbought unloved teddy bears
that taper for a while upwards
through rust-coloured depths
where dirt flowers unfurl
as fine as unworn satin.

Found Poem

Unable to find the remaining cantos, thinking the work unfinished, Dante's son Iacopo resolved to finish his father's work, that it might not go imperfect.

– Boccaccio's *Life of Dante*

i.

Awake too late thinking
Dad's last days his best:

those blank noons
when he'd lean against

the scrubbed wood lintel
framing rubble, shore scree.

The words swam with light –
and then nothing further.

The rest left on a boat
that shuttles between

one nowhere and another.
So his final lines jounce

around in the dry cool dark
underneath the deck.

ii.

Walks bring him back.
His pilled wool cap.

His creased-page face.
His stoop. His boxer's nose.

How he'd snap brambles,
then hold them up

so I could watch
the freed water steam.

iii.

Tonight if I drop off at all
let a dream come of him

calling me out to see rain
frozen in a half moon

to the tarp over his boat.
Water traces the veins

in his fingers. Ghost maps
float upright inside the ice.

Let those worlds fall
and shatter me awake.

Let the rest of his poem
shape itself backwards

out of the glass-clear smash,
out of shards sliding over stone.

After Catullus

Gull-yawk, river water ribbed with gold,
nick of woodsmoke, evening's coal
all soft lit collapsings. Back ache:
a slow treacly leak. Head empty
as the rucksack just now tipped out
with a big luff and shudder
into the wicker laundry basket.

Home: a mattress that catches
the impress of each bone of you,
absorbs your gammy shoulder's click,
cushions the grunt and settle
of gristle and muscle.

Count the eye step by step
down the red plush
altar: amber fang of pickled garlic;
a wax miniature of Spinoza's death-mask;
a cork-stoppered vial of ash in water;
and two bonsai, one oak, one linden,
knotted at the roots.

Guided Meditation App (Final Paywall)

vii.

Picture yourself amid
a slow smashed
punctuation of still water –
lakes and fens in long dark shapes:
brackets, commas, hyphens that hold
zero speech or interjection,
nothing only the silt's muttered
considerations dropping
in an unbroken dark sheet
from the fine nervature
of the drowned weeds
to bloom outwards in a cloud.

viii.

It is recommended
that you keep a record
of what you have seen
by letting hot water
drip one steaming bead
at a time from a pipette
onto the blank
pages at the back
until you are not
really writing, not
writing at all, in fact,
you're printing marks
of punctuation

in raised wavery dimples
of soaked paper
that could pass for snow,
really, if you think of it,
and you're just watching
a calligraphy of steam
shift and unkink
vanishing into the air
of the room you've been
all along, all alone, at last.

Nausikaa

Waking   head pillowed on wavemelt

struggled upright   nets a kilt

stuck to me   fingernails clucked against nylon

flotsam washed in all around

tripod   telephoto lens: Matryoshka of black shells

steel for a set of ribs   plastic for a hull

Windmills turned on the hill   bleached oars sunk

to mark all journeys' end   I combed

the net kilt into rigging for a wrecked junk

a life raft – no: skiff – rose on the sand

the name spelled in pebbles   fizzed away under seafoam

I turned my back on oceans   took the way inland

Acknowledgements

For everything and more: Quinnie, Hugo, and Eva; and my mother, father, and sister. Laura Cassidy, Eimear Ryan, and Jessica Traynor gave me the surprise of my life in taking on this collection. The editing process has been a joy. My thanks to all three. The two boys in the submersible there. Sean, Lisa, and Novak. James and Aimee. Dean Browne. Jan Carson. Michael O'Loughlin. France Jaigu. Tiffany Atkinson. Luke Kennard. Ben Pester. Anthony Vahni Capildeo. May-Lan Tan. Dylan, Lily, and Finn. Robin Myers, John Z. Komurki, and Mariana Rodríguez for helping me restart the motor. Georgie Folan and Leeanne Quinn. Will and Nina. Wendy Erskine. Cathy Sweeney. Diego and Lu. Toby Ryan. Aliana Santana. Jack and Rae. Pepa and all at faber llull. Nora and everyone at CCI. Beatrice Monti della Corte and all at the Santa Maddalena Foundation (yes, you, too, Cloclo). Tommy and Matt. Fede Andornino. City Animal. My first poetry teacher, Kyle Sutton. Aidan McMahon. 'Nausikaa' was written in Chris Kitson's apartment, late 2014: big thanks to him for this and for so much more.

Thank you to the editors of the following journals and anthologies for publishing early versions of some of these poems: *Poetry Ireland Review, Banshee, gorse, The Lighthouse, The Rialto, Ambit, The North, Butcher's Dog, The Quietus, Magma, The London Magazine, Hotel, Propel, Channel, Poets for Gaza, Abridged, 14 Magazine, Gulder, Neurological, Brixton Review of Books, Firmament, Bareknuckle Poet, diSONARE, Squawk Back, Barcelona INK, Icarus*. Will Ford and Nina Hervé at Rough Trade included *Rory Gallagher – Live! – from the Hotel of the Dead* in their Night Life series.

Anselm McDonnell wrote a choral setting for section 15 of the same poem. Titled *Gallagher,* his piece won the Seán Ó Ríada Composition Award in May 2024. In September 2015, the BBC broadcast a recording of 'Where I Come From', after Horacio Lozano Warpola. He is remembered here.

The author gratefully acknowledges the support of the Arts Council.

BANSHEE
PRESS

Banshee Press was founded by writers Laura Cassidy, Claire Hennessy and Eimear Ryan. Since 2015, *Banshee* literary journal has published twice a year. In 2021, Jessica Traynor joined Banshee Press as poetry editor.

The Banshee Press publishing imprint launched in 2019, publishing the very best in new fiction, poetry and memoir. Banshee Press authors include Bebe Ashley, Dylan Brennan, Lucy Sweeney Byrne, Gustav Parker Hibbett, Claire-Lise Kieffer, Mary Morrissy, Deirdre Sullivan, Rosamund Taylor and David Toms.

WWW.BANSHEEPRESS.ORG